Biomes

Grasslands

Malcolm Penny

Chrysalis Children's Books

BIOMES

DESERTS
GRASSLANDS
OCEANS
RAINFORESTS
WETLANDS

Produced by Monkey Puzzle Media Ltd
Gissing's Farm, Fressingfield, Suffolk IP21 5SH, UK

First published in the UK in 2003 by
(*) Chrysalis Children's Books
64 Brewery Road, London N7 9NT

Editor: Andrew Solway
Editorial Manager: Joyce Bentley
Designer: Victoria Webb
Consultant: Michael Allaby
Picture Researcher: Glass Onion Pictures

ISBN: 1 84138 874 2

British Library Cataloguing in Publication Data for this book is available from the British Library.

A BELITHA BOOK

Printed in Hong Kong / China
10 9 8 7 6 5 4 3 2 1

Picture Acknowledgements
We wish to thank the following individuals and organizations for their help and assistance, and for supplying material in their collections: Ecoscene 6 (Andrew Brown), 19 (Frank Blackburn), 22 (Andrew Brown), 23 (Peter Currell), 40 (Pearl Bocknall), 43, 47 (Alan Towse); FLPA *front cover* (David Hosking), 4 (J McDonald/Sunset), 9 (Dembinsky), 11 (Tony Wharton), 12 (Minden Pictures), 14 (S Maslowski), 16 (Winfried Wisniewski), 24 (Tony Wharton), 25 (Neil Bowman), 26 (Minden Pictures), 34 (Fritz Polking), 35 (Leonard Lee Rue), 37 (J C Allen), 39 (S, D and R Maslowski), 42 (David Hosking), 46 (David Hosking); NHPA 18 (David Woodfall), 21 (Jane Gifford); Papilio 17 (John Farmar); Science Photo Library 8 (James King-Holmes), 45 (D A Peel); Still Pictures 1 (Mark Edwards), 3 (Michel Denis-Huot), 5 top (Adrian Arbib), 5 middle (Daniel Dancer), 5 bottom (Mark Edwards), 10 (Gilles Nicolet), 13 (Fritz Polking), 15 (Don Reid), 20 (Mark Edwards), 27 (Adrian Arbib), 28 (Mark Edwards), 29 (Mark Edwards), 30 (Nigel Dickenson), 31 (Mark Edwards), 32 (Thomas Raupach), 33 (Mark Edwards), 36 (Mark Edwards), 38 (Michel Denis-Huot), 41 (Jim Wark), 44 (Roger de la Harpe). Artwork by Michael Posen. The pictures used in this book do not show the actual people named in the case studies in the text.

CONTENTS

Miguel's Story

Miguel Ramirez lives in Argentina. He is a man of the grasslands. Today he is driving into Buenos Aires to deliver vegetables to the market. His route goes past large houses on the outskirts of the city where people are busy cutting their lawns. 'What a waste! They could be turning the grass into beef, not throwing it away in heaps at the bottom of the garden.' Producing beef is Miguel's main job. His wife and eldest daughter grow the vegetables he delivers.

'I LIVE ON the humid pampa, the huge grassland to the south of the city, on a small ranch that I rent from a local landowner. I buy bullock calves to rear on the open pasture, and sell them as beef cattle when they are nearly two years old. After paying for the beasts and their veterinary bills, and buying seeds and pesticides for the vegetable plots, I have enough left over to send my three youngest children to school in the city. They board there during the week, and come home at weekends. My children's schoolfriends live among the noisy, crowded streets of the city. My kids would like to stay more often in the city, where the music scene is loud and lively, and they can eat hamburgers – maybe made from my own beef!

Juan, my eldest son, has finished school, and helps me around the ranch while he waits to go to college next year. He will study art and architecture. "Anything but farming," he says. "I've had enough of that, and there's no future in it for me". He's a disappointment to me. His older sister, Bettina, is different. She's a talented cellist, she plays in an amateur orchestra in the city, but she is happy to live on the ranch. One day she will marry, but for now she loves the life on the land, working with her mother in their little fields of melons, cucumbers and tomatoes. "The sky goes on forever," she says, "and I can hear the music of the wind and the birds. When I marry, it will be to a farmer, so that I can live out here in the open. I love the pampa". She's like me and her mother. These wide open spaces are our home. We're not rich, but we are happy, living where our fathers and grandfathers did – and in much the same way.'

Problems in other grasslands

Miguel's cattle graze on grasslands that in the past supported many different wild animals. All over the world, grasslands have been taken over by people, to grow food or raise farm animals.

WILD SURVIVORS
Among the few surviving wild grasslands are the plains of Mongolia. Wandering herdsmen, graze their cattle and horses there. Wild grassland also survives in East Africa, where the savannah grasslands have been preserved in national parks.

NORTH AMERICA
In all but a few areas of the North American prairies the grasslands are a human domain. The grasses have been ploughed up and turned into farmland. Farmers use machines to plant, grow and harvest wheat, maize and other crops.

AUSTRALIA
In the Australian outback, most of the grassland has been taken over by huge sheep and cattle stations. The sheep or cattle eat all the grass, leaving little for kangaroos, wallabies and other wild inhabitants.

What Are Grasslands?

Grasslands are the most widespread biome on land, covering one-fifth of the land surface. They are areas where grasses are the dominant plants. There are relatively few species of grasses, but each grows in huge numbers, densely packed together. Directly or indirectly, grasses provide a very large proportion of human food.

A sea of grass: short-grass prairie, Colorado, USA.

RASSLANDS FIRST APPEARED about 65 million years ago, in the Cenozoic era. This was a time when the Earth's climate was becoming cooler and drier. Grasslands cover land that is too dry to support trees, which need a damp climate, but is not so dry as to be desert. The main types of grassland are temperate and tropical grasslands. Temperate grasslands include the prairies of North America, the pampas of Argentina and the cool steppes of eastern Europe and Asia. Tropical grasslands range from the Sahel, where sparse clumps of grass struggle to survive among stunted bushes on sandy

What is a biome?

A biome is major regional community of plants and animals, with similar life forms and environmental conditions. Each biome is named after its dominant feature, for instance tropical rainforest or grassland.

ground, to the vast Australian outback and the East African savannah, an open grassy plain dotted with trees.

How do grasslands survive?

Even in an ideal climate, grasslands cannot survive without regular disturbance. The most common is fire, started by lightning during a dry period. Unless grasslands are periodically burned, shrubs and trees invade them. If the trees are far enough apart the area is savannah, a form of grassland, but when the trees grow closely the grass cannot get enough sunlight to grow, and woodland takes over. Fire kills off tree saplings, but grass quickly recovers from burning.

The other factor that keeps grasslands open is grazing. Herds of millions of wildebeest in Africa eat and trample tree seedlings before they can grow. (In the past, herds of bison did the same job on the North American prairies.) The grazers eat the grasses, but this does not kill the grass plants.

Do people help grasslands survive?

Some grasslands were created and maintained by people from prehistoric times. The North American prairies were kept open by Native American hunters. Observing that animals came to feed on the fresh shoots after a natural fire, they realised that they could attract animals to hunt by starting fires themselves. Other grasslands are maintained as pastures by people grazing livestock. They are classified as man-made or semi-natural, as opposed to wild or natural grasslands.

Why are grasslands so fertile?

Grasses grow in places with moderate rainfall, so the nutrients in the soil are not washed away by heavy rain. They build up deep, rich topsoil, and their roots hold the soil in place: even after a flood, the nutrients remain. Natural grasslands feed huge herds of grazing animals, and their droppings fertilise the grass. But trying to feed too many animals, or grow too much food on grasslands can cause serious damage.

Solid soil

In contrast to the loose leaf-litter on the floor of a forest, grassland soil is trodden down by the hooves of grazing animals and interwoven with grass roots. The total length of roots under a square metre of prairie is 38 km. Some prairie grasses have deep roots, which are useful in times of drought. These may reach down 3–4.5 m.

The green shading on this map shows the world's major grassland areas.

What Happens In Grasslands?

The activity in grasslands takes place at three levels – on a tiny scale below the surface, on a larger scale among the grass stems, and on an even larger scale above ground, where grazing animals and their predators live. All three levels are rich and complex habitats.

UNDERGROUND, THE DENSE mat of grass roots is home to vast numbers of burrowing creatures. These include many different species of small roundworms called nematodes. A cubic foot of soil contains about half a million nematodes. Some are predators, but most are herbivores, eating the roots of the grass. Nematodes need large amounts of food for their size, and combined with their vast numbers this means that nematodes, not wildebeest or other grazing animals, are the main plant-eaters in grasslands.

In addition to nematodes, grassland soil contains huge numbers of insect larvae, mites, and other tiny organisms. They play an important part in maintaining the grassland, by breaking down animal and plant wastes into useful nutrients that enrich the soil.

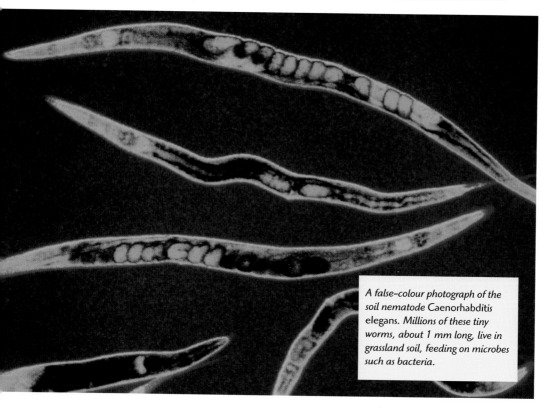

A false-colour photograph of the soil nematode Caenorhabditis elegans. Millions of these tiny worms, about 1 mm long, live in grassland soil, feeding on microbes such as bacteria.

Black-eyed Susan flowers are the tallest 'trees' in this miniature forest of prairie plants.

What happens at ground level?

To the animals that live among the stems, grasslands are a forest, a pasture and hunting ground as rich as the tropical rainforests. Mice and voles are the plant-eaters. Weasels and stoats are the top predators (hunters), but there are also carnivorous beetles and centipedes, hunting insects and small molluscs. Just above the ground, birds chase insects and gather seeds.

What can we see above ground level?

The large-scale action on the open African savannah is well known, from countless TV wildlife shows. The savannah can be dangerous for prey animals, but it is an easy place to make exciting films. Predators hunt there, and huge herds of grazers wander in search of water and fresh grazing. Crocodiles lurk in the rivers, snatching the migrants as they pass. The herds of wildebeest can be a million strong.

It is difficult to imagine today, but herds as vast as the wildebeest herds in Africa once wandered the North American prairies. At their peak, the prairies were home to 60–70 million bison and 50 million pronghorn antelope. They were preyed on by wolves, bears, mountain lions – and by people.

A bush fire is an alarming sight, but grass soon burns out, and the fire is not hot enough to cause serious damage.

What makes grasses special plants?

The most important feature of grasses is that unlike most plants they grow from the base, not from an apical shoot (one at the top of the plant). When a grazing animal bites off their leaves, grasses continue to grow from a central bud very close to the ground, fuelled by underground food stores. Being cut off near the ground actually stimulates grass to grow, as anyone will know who has a lawn to look after. This enables grasslands to flourish when it is being heavily grazed, or after being burned.

When do grasses grow?

In the tropics, grasses grow during and shortly after the rains, or in some places in the short time when the ground is not flooded. In temperate regions grasses grow best in the spring, between a cool, wet winter and a hot, dry summer. Where the summers are not so hot or dry, as in much of Europe, grasses grow throughout the summer months. As soon as conditions are right, they use their underground energy stores to produce shoots, grow fast, flower and produce seeds. When the seeds have ripened and been dispersed, and if the grass has not been cropped by grazing animals, the top material dies back, leaving the ground covered in a 'thatch' of dead grass. Left alone, this would smother new growth in the following season, and slow down the warming of the ground by spring sunshine in temperate regions. In wild grassland, autumn fires clear away the thatch.

Why don't fires destroy grasslands?

Wild fires are spectacular and often frightening events. In forests they can be very dangerous, threatening human homes and lives as well as the animals that live in the forest, and often causing serious damage. Forest fires are difficult to control, because the dense fuel generates a lot of heat. Grass fires are different: the light fuel burns fast and is soon gone, so that the fire is short and relatively cool. The blackened, smoking ground after the fire looks like a disaster, but many of the animals can run or fly away, and the grass is not seriously harmed. Fresh shoots soon appear, and the cycle can begin all over again.

Grevy's zebra is the biggest of the three species of zebra. It lives on dry grasslands in Ethiopia, Somalia and northern Kenya. In the south, its range overlaps with the more common plains zebra.

Grassland gardeners

Earthworms swallow large quantities of soil, to extract bacteria and other single-celled organisms for food. They then pass the soil out of their bodies at the surface as worm casts. This process turns over the soil and aerates it. It is amazing that on the North American prairie, the earthworms weigh more than the bison did at their peak. In pastureland in Europe, there is a greater weight of worms per acre than of cattle and sheep.

Another important group of soil-turners, moving as much soil as the earthworms, are harvester ants. These ants build large underground colonies, excavating the soil grain by grain.

How Do Animals Live In Grasslands?

Grazing animals, large and small, find an easy living on grasslands. They are surrounded by food as far as the eye can see. They are also surrounded by predators, from lions and pumas that hunt antelope and deer to jackals and coyotes that feed on mice and other small rodents. The key link in this long and complex food chain is the grass that indirectly feeds them all.

WHEN GRASSLANDS DEVELOPED in the Cenozoic era, many animals evolved to exploit the new biome. Horses, which had until then been small woodland animals, became large, swift runners. Antelope evolved into many different grass-eaters, some more specialized than others. Much later, a group of woodland primates emerged on to the plains to become savannah hunters and food-gatherers. They eventually evolved into the genus *Homo* – human beings.

How are animals adapted for grazing?

There is an enormous range of animals that live by grazing, from nimble deer and antelope to ponderous white rhinoceroses and elephants. Horses, too, are highly adapted as grazing animals. Most rely on being able to see long distances and run fast to evade their predators (rhinos and elephants are exceptions), but above all they must be able to eat and digest grass. Grass stems contain silicon, a tough mineral that wears away teeth. So grazing animals have flat grinding teeth with hard ridges of enamel that are very hard-wearing. Many have a way of replacing these teeth when they do eventually wear out.

When grasslands emerged, horses were transformed from small, shy woodland creatures into swift runners of the open plains. These wild mustangs live in Montana, USA.

A cheetah hunts a Thomson's gazelle. The grass that fed the gazelle will indirecty feed the cheetah too.

How do animals digest grass?

The cell walls of plants, including grass, are made of a tough substance called cellulose. No mammal can digest cellulose directly. To extract energy from plant food, they need help from bacteria, which break down the cellulose for them. This process, called fermentation, works in one of two ways.

Most large grazing animals deal with grass by rumination. They have a stomach divided into four chambers. They grind up the grass and swallow it into the first chamber (the rumen), where fermentation softens the grass blades. A little later, they regurgitate their food and grind it again, a process known as 'chewing the cud'. When they next swallow it, it is fine enough to pass through the sieve-like second chamber and into the third and fourth chambers, where it is fermented further. The bacteria take some energy for themselves, but there is plenty left over for the owner of the stomach.

Rumination is very efficient, but slow. Antelope, deer, cattle, sheep, goats, camels and giraffes are all ruminants. Horses, rhinos and tapirs use a different process, called cecal digestion. Their fermentation chamber is a large bag called the cecum, between the small and large intestines. They pack it with grass, and wait for the bacteria to break it down. However, they do not wait very long: food passes through a horse in 48 hours, whereas it takes 70–90 hours in a cow. A horse extracts only 70 per cent as much energy from its food as a cow. By processing larger amounts of food more quickly, it can gather the same total amount of energy.

How does grass feed predators?

Grassland predators like lions and cheetahs don't eat grass, but they are just as dependent on it for their food as grazing animals. They let the grazing animals digest the grass, and then eat the grazers. Humans also rely on grass indirectly: they use cattle and sheep to change grass into meat and milk.

A long-tailed weasel in its white winter fur catches a meadow mouse that had been forced by hunger to leave the safety of its burrow.

How can prey animals avoid being eaten?

Wild prey animals have evolved a series of defensive measures to help avoid predators, based mainly on being very alert. Grassland prey animals have good hearing, a keen sense of smell and a wide field of vision. They are very quick off the mark when danger threatens, and many species can outrun a predator over long distances. Domestic animals by contrast have been bred to be slow and placid, and to trust people. Some grassland animals avoid predators by living underground. Badgers spend the daylight hours in large burrows called setts. Moles hunt earthworms in the soil, and very rarely come to the surface at all. Rabbits, gophers and prairie dogs live in huge, complex underground burrow systems, usually emerging to feed at dusk and during the night. The African and European equivalents of prairie dogs are mongooses and marmots. Marmots are rodents, related to squirrels.

Why are rodents important?

Rodents are an important group of grassland mammals, partly because they serve as prey for smaller carnivores such as hawks, eagles, coyotes, jackals and foxes. Rodents feed mainly on seeds, but many of them also hunt insects among the grass stems. They serve as a link between the grass at the base of the food chain and predators that are not big enough to catch large grazing animals such as antelope.

What insects live in grasslands?

Insects are the most successful and varied group of animals in grasslands. Butterflies are very numerous; they feed and breed on wildflowers, not grasses. Grasshoppers and crickets are members of an enormous family, with 17 000 known species, most of them tropical or subtropical. Their bodies are heavily armoured against predators with a tough material called chitin. They also have long, powerful hind legs for leaping to safety, and if all else fails they can fly away.

Do all grassland insects eat plants?

Another very successful group of grassland insects feeds on other animals rather than on plants. They are the blood-sucking flies. Some, like botflies, have a complex life cycle. Their eggs are swallowed by grazing animals and develop inside their guts, often causing great distress and sometimes death. Others simply land on their victims and suck their blood. Horseflies are highly adapted to this way of feeding. They fly silently, and land very softly, so that the first their victim knows of their arrival is the sharp pain of the bite – by which time the damage is done.

Why are dung beetles important?

A vital group of insects where so many large mammals eat grass is the dung beetles. Without them, grasslands would be buried in a layer of droppings so deep that nothing could grow. The adults eat some of the dung, but their larvae (young) account for most of it. Some parent beetles simply lay their eggs in dung piles, while others dig a burrow to bury dung for their larvae to eat when they hatch. Some make large balls of dung, which they roll to the burrow: others simply collect it in mouthfuls. Dung beetles have many predators, including storks and ibises, which probe dung piles in search of the large, luscious larvae.

Locusts, members of the grasshopper family, are very successful plant–eaters in grasslands. Much of the time they are dull coloured and live and feed alone. But some are brightly coloured, like this one from the grasslands of Madagascar. On the African mainland locusts form huge swarms, which can seriously damage food crops.

What birds live in grasslands?

Grassland birds are mostly seed-eaters, and they often use grass blades to weave their nests. The most successful of all is the red-billed quelea, a small finch that lives in Africa. It moves in enormous flocks, often more than a million strong, migrating across country to follow the rains. It is the most numerous species of bird on earth: the population is estimated at 1500 million. Although each bird weighs only 20g, and eats only 2.5g

A flock of red–billed quelea. Quelea flocks are so dense, and make so much noise with their wings, that they drive even elephants away from waterholes when they come down to drink.

of seeds a day, a large flock can strip the seeds from an area of grass or crops in a very short time. Their colonies of woven grass nests are so huge that they sometimes break the branches of savannah trees.

Are there any flightless birds?

Grassland plains are also the home to several species of large flightless birds such as ostriches, rheas, emus, bustards and cassowaries.

Wild ostriches are now found only in Africa. They used to live in Syria and Arabia as well, but the last one outside Africa was killed in 1941.

Rheas, which live in South American grasslands, differ from ostriches in having three toes instead of two. The rhea population has fallen considerably in recent years. Rheas and their eggs are often eaten by local people, and they are killed to be used as dog food. Rheas near agricultural areas are also killed, because they will eat almost any crop.

Emus in Australia also have three toes – they still survive in spite of fierce persecution during the early twentieth century, when many emus were killed with machine guns to protect growing wheat.

What about birds of prey?

The secretary bird, which lives on the African savannah, is not flightless but spends most of its time on the ground. It hunts snakes on foot, stamping them to death with long, armoured legs. Other birds of prey search the sea of grass from the air, looking for small mammals or reptiles such as lizards and snakes.

Some birds of prey prefer to eat carrion (dead meat). African vultures soar over the grasslands watching for carrion. In the southern United States and Central America, huge condors are the American equivalent of vultures.

DEBATE – Should local people eat threatened birds such as rheas?

- Yes. Because the loss of bird habitat is the biggest problem, not local people eating the birds.
- No. Because when a bird population is threatened, even the small numbers eaten by local people have an effect.

A secretary bird in Kenya eats a venomous puff adder. Its long legs, covered in thick, shiny scales, protect it from the snake's fangs.

Are Grasslands Permanent?

Many grasslands have existed for thousands of years, but this does not mean that they are permanent. To survive, they need constant intervention by outside forces, such as drought, fire or grazing animals. This makes them very suitable for use by humans – and vulnerable to misuse.

IN BOTANICAL TERMS, a climax community is one whose members may change as time passes and the environment changes, but which remains essentially the same. Forests and seashores are climax communities, but grasslands are not. If fires no longer happen, for instance, or if grazing animals disappear, grassland will give way to a different type of vegetation.

The process of development of the plant community in an area is called succession. The best way to see succession in action is to clear a plot of land and watch what happens over a period of years. One group of plants flourishes and is succeeded by another, then another, until eventually a steady state is reached. This is the climax community for that area.

An old quarry near Birmingham, England, which was colonised by quick-growing birch trees about twenty years after it was abandoned.

A new plantation of hardwood trees in Surrey, England, makes an ideal habitat for foxgloves; pioneer plants that flourish in open, sunny places.

What are 'pioneer plants'?

The first plants to appear on a cleared plot of land are known as 'pioneer plants'. These are species whose seeds are widely dispersed, perhaps by wind or animals, and germinate wherever they land. In a garden, pioneer plants are called weeds. Nettles, docks, thistles, bindweeds – and grasses – are common pioneer plants in a temperate climate. They are mostly annuals, and they do not survive competition from other plants for long. Left untended, cleared land will quickly become mainly grassland, as the grasses overcome and outlive most of the other pioneer plants.

What happens next?

This is not the end of the story. After perhaps three or four years, more competitive plants begin to grow, such as perennial herbs and shrubs. They are invaded in their turn by the seedlings of quick-growing trees such as birch and ash. After about fifty years have passed, the cleared plot will have become shady woodland. The succession is still not complete, however, because seedlings of other trees, such as beech and oak, are adapted to grow in these conditions, and they can outgrow and outlive the first arrivals. After another fifty or a hundred years, the area will be a stable forest of beech, oak and ash, the climax community of temperate lowlands. Any change that takes place from now on will be very slow, in a complex ecosystem dominated by long-lived, highly competitive trees.

When does grassland persist?

For grassland to become established and to persist for any length of time, something has to happen to stop it turning into woodland. We have already seen the way in which fire, drought or grazing can damage or kill many of the plants that compete with the grass, such as trees and shrubs. The grass, on the other hand, can usually survive these things.

Not all the plants that compete with grasses are wiped out by drought, fires and grazing. Many species of wildflower survive successfully in grasslands. In fact, three-quarters of grassland plant species are not grasses. Orchids, daisies, buttercups, campions and knapweeds are just some of the many kinds of wildflower found on temperate grasslands around the world. Orchids are also found in tropical grasslands.

Clearing land for crops in Sri Lanka. By cutting and burning woodland, people produce conditions where grasses will grow – in this case cereals that they will use for food. This process, called 'slash and burn', is one of the oldest ways of preparing land for agriculture.

How do non-grass plants survive?

Plants that survive in grasslands must have a way of overcoming the threats to their existence. Fire and drought, both of which wipe out tree seedlings, have less effect on plants that have deep storage roots. Thistles are a good example of such plants. They have long, fleshy roots from which they can re-grow after being burned away by fire, or shrivelled by drought. Docks and nettles have the same type of storage roots. Nettle roots wander long distances under the ground, and can push up new shoots far from the parent plant.

If such plants are eaten by grazers (or if their tops are cut off by a lawnmower) they quickly grow new leaves. The new leaves make more food to pack into the plant's storage roots, ready for the next time the plant is damaged.

Thistles are defended in other ways against grazing animals. They are covered in fine spines, which are painful to sensitive lips. Furthermore, they can grow flat against the ground, so that fire – and the lawnmower - passes over them and leaves them undamaged.

Other grassland survivors avoid being eaten by having a foul taste: some of them are actually poisonous to grazing animals. Ragworts and hemlock, for example, are poisonous to many grazers.

In a well-grown hayfield, thistles have to grow tall, to flower and produce seeds. Where the grass is grazed or mowed, thistles have to grow flat against the ground to survive.

What are other ways of surviving?

Some plants are not protected by spines or stings, and their leaves and flowers taste good to grazing animals. Plants like this survive until they have flowered and produced seeds by growing quickly with their leaves flat against the ground. The many members of the daisy and dandelion family grow like this, and are very successful survivors in grazed grassland.

Some plants can only survive in grassland that is grazed: if the grass is allowed to grow tall, they do not receive enough light, and die out. Many low-growing daisies are like this, as are a number of rare and decorative plants such as orchids. Other plants can only survive if the grasses grow tall. Some types of tall daisies such as marguerites, and vetches and red poppies are plants that like tall grass. Tall-growing plants like these are common weeds of grain crops. However, when grass is cut for hay or for silage, such 'weeds' are a welcome addition. Hay is mature grass cut and dried to be stored as feed for cattle, and silage is made by cutting grass and fermenting it to produce valuable winter feed.

Dandelions and daisies are among the first flowers to appear in pasture land. They grow in the spring while the grass is still short.

What defences does grass have?

We have seen how its deep root system protects prairie grass against damage by fire and drought. But other grasses have a dense, tangled mat of shallow roots, so how do they survive fires?

In fact, grass fires do not usually overheat any more than the top few centimetres of soil, so even grasses with shallow roots can survive. A tangled mat of roots is useful in surviving a drought, because the matted roots hold enough water to keep the grass alive until the rains return.

Tall grass, as in this grain field in West Sussex, England, is the preferred habitat for poppies. They are spectacular and beautiful, but farmers regard them as a weed.

Grasses offer no defence against being grazed. As we have seen, they actually grow best when they are regularly cut or nibbled close to the ground. Grasses are proof against all the forces that hold back the competition. As long as those forces keep up the pressure, grasslands can survive in their incomplete stage of succession. This is what has made grasslands, in all their various forms, the most widespread biome on Earth.

How Does Climate Affect Grasslands?

Grasslands can grow in a broad range of climates. Climate also affects the way in which people use grasslands. As well as the temperate prairies and the tropical savannahs, there are some very specialised grasslands dotted round the world.

TYPICAL GRASSLAND SPREADS across rolling or flat country, away from the coast, in areas with moderate rainfall. Tropical grasslands grow in a climate that has wet and dry seasons, the dry season being the equivalent of the cold winter in colder climates. Temperate grasslands, such as the North American prairies, do not have such a pronounced dry season. In temperate grasslands the diversity of plant species is much less than in the tropics.

Why do tropical grasslands have trees?

In the tropics, trees have evolved that can withstand both grazing pressure and fire, so the grassland here is dotted with trees. This kind of grassland is known as savannah.

The acacia in Africa is a good example of a savannah tree. Its thorny branches have been described as being like a salad made with barbed wire. Few animals can get round the acacia's spiny defences. Giraffes, with their long,

A giraffe uses its flexible tongue to pick fresh leaves from among the thorns of an acacia tree.

nimble tongues, can pick acacia leaves from between the thorns, while black rhinos have leathery mouths that can crunch up the thorniest twigs. Trees like this are dotted over African grasslands, and tropical grasslands in general.

Paramo pastures in Venezuela offer good grazing for hardy cattle in summer. Every autumn, the cattle are rounded up on horseback and taken down to the valley for the winter.

What is paramo grassland?

In the high Andes of South America, between the subtropical rainforest that reaches to about 1800m and the snowline above 5000m, there is a temperate zone. The higher parts of this zone, between about 4000m and 5000m, support an area of alpine grassland called the paramo.

At this altitude it is very cold during the day, and freezing every night. The vegetation is short grass dotted with a variety of tiny, often brightly coloured flowers. This dramatic scenery, where cliffs and gullies divide the rolling grassland, is used by farmers to graze hardy mountain cattle.

What are the pampas?

Most of eastern Argentina in South America consists of huge flat grassy plains called the pampas. The greater part of the plain, known as the dry pampa, is a salty, sandy wilderness. However, the eastern edge of the pampas, called the humid pampa, is cooler and well-watered. When Spanish settlers arrived in the region, they raised cattle and herds of semi-wild horses on the humid pampa. Gauchos, the famous cowboys of the plains, tended the cattle and horses. Today, the pampa is devoted mainly to growing wheat, maize and alfalfa. These crops are used to supplement the grazing for herds of pedigree cattle and sheep.

A pair of royal albatrosses at their nest, sheltered among the tussock grass on South Island, New Zealand.

What is tussock grassland?

Tussock grasslands grow in New Zealand and on some of the islands just outside the Antarctic Circle, such as South Georgia, Bird Island and the Falklands. A similar form of grassland grows in the tropics, but only on the top of high mountains. Tussock grass, as its name suggests, grows in dense clumps or tussocks, often as much as 2m tall. It grows in this way because it has never been grazed by mammals. It is easy to imagine the impact of introducing animals like sheep and deer to previously untouched areas of tussock grassland: large areas have been completely destroyed.

What is overgrazing?

Raising domestic cattle on enclosed areas of grassland is a relatively new development in agriculture. It can cause damage to the pasture known as 'overgrazing', in which the grass is grazed and the ground trampled beyond recovery. Wild grazing animals, or domestic herds that are allowed to range widely over large areas, do not cause such harm to grasslands. The way animals are grazed in Mongolia is a good example of how overgrazing can be avoided.

What happens on the Mongolian plains?

Mongolia is a country of grasslands, where huge plains cover four-fifths of the country. The plains are the home of a wandering nomadic people. They raise herds of sheep, goats and cattle, which they tend on horseback. When the animals have eaten the grazing in a particular area, the herders move them to new pastures.

Mongolian herders set up a village of yurts, then graze their animals in groups according to species (sheep, horses and cattle are taken out separately). The animals graze through the day, working in a spiral out from the village, and are brought back at night. When the journey

A Mongolian herdsman dismantles the frame of his yurt, ready to move with his family and their herds to new pastures.

to the pasture becomes too long for convenience, the whole village packs up and moves to a new location. This protects the grasslands from overgrazing. For many centuries the nomads' animals have provided them with dairy products, meat, blood, wool and leather. However, this might be coming to an end.

What is happening in Mongolia now?

Like most nomads, the Mongol herders do not pay much attention to material possessions, or to modern developments in the world beyond the plains. Governments have tried to persuade the herders to settle on farms and ranches, where they can be provided with schools, hospitals and modern communications. Some of the nomads are reluctant to leave their traditional life – they would prefer to slaughter some of their animals to supply the livestock industry, while still maintaining their wandering way of life. Traditionally, Mongol herders refuse to eat vegetables and despise any occupation that cannot be carried out on horseback. In one area a herd of horses had to be kept specially to provide fermented milk to factory workers, because they refused to work without it.

DEBATE - Should nomadic herding give way to a modern, settled way of life?

- No. Because wandering herds do less damage to the grasslands, and the ancient nomadic culture is worth preserving.
- Yes. Because everyone has a right to education, healthcare and modern communications, and a duty to contribute to the local economy.

How Do Humans Use Grasslands?

When early humans first wandered on the grassy plains, they were hunter-gatherers, finding food where they could. It would be more than a million years before they hit on the idea of planting crops or rearing domestic animals. The first humans to realise that grass seeds are edible discovered a source of food that has been mankind's staple diet ever since.

MOST HUMAN POPULATIONS grow their food on relatively well-watered grasslands that they have adapted for their own use. All cereals are modified grasses. They are bred over many generations to produce larger seeds, which remain on the plant after ripening rather than being shed as they are by wild grasses. Drier grasslands have been used for thousands of years to raise domestic cattle.

Harvesting irrigated rice by hand in Burkina Faso, West Africa.

These rice terraces in Bali may have been cut into the hillside more than a thousand years ago. Small channels allow water to trickle from each terrace to the one below. However, in dry weather water must be carried by hand to the topmost terraces.

How did farming start?

Humans began farming in the Middle East about ten thousand years ago, in an area now known as the Fertile Crescent, a hilly, grassy region that curves round the northern edge of the Arabian Desert. A group of hunter-gatherers may have realised that plants grow from seeds, and, in a daring experiment, buried some of their hard-earned collection of wild barley. Or perhaps they were saving the barley to eat later, and returned to find that it had sprouted.

Independently, people planted rice in Asia, and maize and squashes in America. However they began, these first farmers changed the course of human history. When they no longer had to roam in search of seeds to eat, they could settle in villages. They could tame the wild sheep and goats on the surrounding hills, so that they no longer had to go hunting. Farming had begun.

What was the impact of early farmers?

When people began growing crops and rearing livestock, they found that they had enemies all around. Inedible plants threatened to choke their crops, and bugs and birds ate them. Predators came to steal their sheep and goats. The farmers rooted out the weeds, and did what they could to discourage the pests and drive away or kill the predators.

When they had filled all the available grassland with their crops and pastures, early farmers made more space by clearing woodlands, digging irrigation ditches and carving terraces (stepped fields) into hillsides. They left their mark on the face of the Earth.

In some places where hillsides were terraced, today's farmers still grow crops on the ancient terraces, which have been in place for hundreds, if not thousands, of years.

What effect have later farmers had?

The arrival of Europeans on the plains of North America is the most extreme example of the impact of farming on grasslands. The Europeans were already established farmers, and they quickly displaced the Native Americans, who were mainly hunter-gatherers. As they did so they transformed the landscape.

Native Americans cultivated crops on a small scale on family plots, but the newcomers grew crops for sale, not just to feed their families. Where the natives had tilled the soil with sharpened sticks, the newcomers used horse-drawn ploughs. Parts of the prairie were too tough even for these ploughs, until John Deere invented the steel plough in 1837 and exposed the wonderfully fertile soil beneath the dense prairie surface.

Where their ancestors plucked out weeds and squashed bugs by hand, leaving many survivors, modern farmers spray herbicides and pesticides over huge areas. This can wipe out huge numbers of insects and other creatures, including harmless or beneficial ones. Humans today can produce cereals and meat in quantities far greater than the old farmers could ever have imagined.

What crops do people grow?

All cereal crops are hybrid grasses (mixtures of more than one type). Wheat, oats and barley are the main cereals in temperate regions, while in warmer countries maize and sorghum

How have farmers affected prairie dogs?

In the past, the prairie dogs in North America played a vital part in maintaining the pasture for the vast herds of bison. Their burrows and droppings aerated and fertilized the land, so that the grass around their burrows ('towns') was of a higher quality. Bison preferrred to graze near prairie dog towns. However, when cattle replaced bison, ranchers poisoned prairie dogs because they believed they competed for the grass, when in fact the higher quality grazing round their towns more than makes up for what they eat. The population of prairie dogs is now about a tenth of what it was before European farmers arrived.

Mechanical harvesting of barley in Berkshire, England.

Sorghum is a grass that grows to more than 3m in height. It is the staple cereal in large areas of China, India and Africa, but the world's largest producer is the USA, where it is grown to feed cattle.

are more important. Rice is the most important cereal in terms of the amount produced, but wheat is more important in terms of world trade.

Not all crops grown on grasslands are modified grasses. Fields of soybeans or tobacco, and plantations of citrus fruits or pineapples cover millions of acres that were once open grasslands, with all their variety of plant and animal life.

Do all domestic animals eat grass?

Grasslands around the world support 3 billion domestic animals – cattle, sheep, goats and camels. Not all of these animals need grass. Goats can flourish by browsing; eating leaves and twigs from trees and shrubs rather than grass. Where overgrazing has degraded the

DEBATE – Should we use herbicides and pesticides to grow crops?

- Yes. These chemicals protect crops and help to produce high yields.
- No. Pesticides and herbicides kill beneficial insects as well as bad ones, and cause pollution.

land, goats may be the only livestock that can find anything to eat. They provide milk and meat for their owners, but they eventually destroy the trees and shrubs, leaving the people without fuel. Keeping goats on overgrazed land is one of the main causes of serious environmental damage.

Why are there so many cattle?

Cattle hold a special place in some cultures. Hindus revere cows, and although they use their milk they are not allowed to kill them. In some African countries, and in Madagascar, cattle are used instead of money, or simply kept as a measure of wealth. A family with a herd of cattle is highly regarded by their neighbours, even though the animals might be close to starving. Cattle are also used as work animals in many parts of the world. They were used that way in Europe until fairly recently.

Cattle are also raised in enormous numbers because of the worldwide demand for beef. Much of this is used to make hamburgers; the rest goes to supermarkets and restaurants in wealthy countries. Raising beef cattle requires grass. Where pastureland has run out, tracts of forest are felled to provide places for the cattle to graze. In the western USA, cattle are also raised in feedlots – they live in small pens, and eat grain that is brought to them.

DEBATE – Should cattle grazing be limited to preserve grasslands?

- No. Because cattle are an important food source, particularly for people in wealthy countries.
- Yes. Because there is no pasture left for wildlife, and many wild species that live on grasslands are disappearing.

Modern veterinary medicine is used to make cattle herds more productive. Antibiotics are given to cattle to keep them healthy even in very crowded conditions, and some cattle are given other drugs to make them grow bigger and more quickly.

Traditional cattle markets in England are still centres for buying and selling on a small, local scale.

Goats are valuable animals for milk, meat and skins in dry regions, because they can live well on poor food, including browse from bushes and shrubs. However, they often aggravate overgrazing.

What should we grow on grasslands?

Growing modified grasses, such as wheat, barley or pulses (plants like lentils, beans and peas), produces more protein per acre than rearing livestock for meat and milk. Also, the other costs associated with producing meat are very high. Producing animal protein uses eight times more food energy than it produces. Producing grain-fed beef uses fifty times more water than producing rice.

On the plus side, animal protein contains a mixture of nutrients and vitamins that cannot be obtained from a single type of food plant. Also, many grassland areas are unsuitable for growing arable crops (for example most of the western side of Britain); in these places, livestock farming is the only type of food production that is feasible. And people like eating meat.

US beef cattle

'Each year an estimated 41 million tons of plant protein is fed to US livestock to produce an estimated 7 million tons of animal protein for human consumption. About 26 million tons of the livestock feed comes from grains, and 15 million tons from forage crops. Thus for every kilogram of high-quality animal protein produced, livestock are fed nearly 6 kg of plant protein.

'More than 302 million hectares of land are devoted to producing feed for the US livestock population – about 272 million hectares in pasture, and 30 million for cultivating feed grains.'

David Pimentel, ecologist, 1997

How Are Humans Causing Change In Grasslands?

Human domination of the world's grasslands has changed most of them from their original condition. A number of animal and plant species have disappeared completely, and others are endangered. Present ways of grazing cattle in developed countries are causing serious harm to grasslands: in many developing countries, this damage is beyond repair.

EVER SINCE FARMING began, humans have changed grasslands to make them suitable for their own uses. Rolling hills covered in flowers and insects have become orderly crop plantations. At first, this happened on a small scale, but when farming became an industry whole landscapes were permanently altered. Inevitably, plants and animals suffered.

Burrowing owls in Florida stand guard over the burrow where their fledgling hatched.

What animals have disappeared?

The first enemies of farmers were the predators that threatened their livestock. Since the earliest times, tigers, lions, pumas and wolves have been under attack from farmers, and as a result such large predators are now rare. They have been protected only in recent times, in remote reserves where they are no threat to farming. In some places, this protection has been almost too successful. Pumas are now protected in North America, and they are multiplying rapidly. Recently there have been a number of attacks on people.

Other animals have come under pressure because they are a nuisance rather than a threat. Prairie dogs undermine cattle ranges, causing accidents when animals fall into the honeycombed ground, and many ranchers poison them to protect their stock. But we have seen that prairie dogs and their 'towns' are an important part of the prairie ecosystem. In Europe, moles have been persecuted as pests in a similar way. Like prairie dogs they undermine the ground, but they can also contaminate silage, causing it to rot rather than produce sweet cattle feed. However, moles are triumphant survivors, even though they have been persecuted for hundreds of years.

What has been the effect on bird life?

Ground-nesting birds are accidental victims of farming. Crop plants are often too tall for them to nest among, and pesticides wipe out the insects they feed on. In pastures, cattle trample their nests and eat the grass that should give them cover. One badly affected species on the North American prairies is the burrowing owl, which needs undisturbed grassland for nesting, and is vulnerable to trampling by cattle. Birds of prey have suffered too, partly because grazing reduces the cover where their prey lives.

In Britain, and possibly other parts of Europe, farmers have changed from sowing cereals in spring to sowing them in winter. This has had a serious effect on ground-nesting birds such as skylarks. These birds need short plants, or stubble, for nesting, but by the time the skylarks nest, winter-sown cereals are too tall. The few suitable breeding areas are overcrowded, and many birds respond by not breeding at all.

Black–tailed prairie dogs are an important part of the ecosystem, but they are often persecuted by farmers,

What has been the effect on plant life?

Ploughing and heavy overgrazing can both destroy plant life. Ploughing destroys the original plant cover completely, especially if it is followed by the regular use of weedkillers. The crop plants that replace the natural plant cover may provide homes for some animals – the harvest mouse in Europe, for example, lives comfortably among tall wheat stems. However, crop plants are of no use to most animal species.

Overgrazing causes more subtle changes. While it is true that grass grows better when it is nibbled off, there is a limit to the damage it can survive. As we have seen, many plants have defences against being eaten. The end result of heavy overgrazing will be that all the edible grasses are gone, leaving behind stands of thistles and docks and other non-edible plants. On the other hand some plants, such as certain species of orchid, are adapted to living on grazed land, so long as it is not overgrazed, and cannot live anywhere else.

Overgrazing has killed the grass and left hard, crusty soil where water cannot soak in – so the trees die as well.

Can endangered animals be saved?

In 1987 the black-footed ferret in Wyoming, USA, a small predator that lives on prairie dogs, was so close to extinction that the last 18 known survivors were taken in and bred in captivity. In 1991, 49 of their descendants were released into their old home, and in 1992 a further 90 were released. They have since bred in the wild, and scientists are now fairly confident that the population will recover.

Where are these effects most serious?

One of the areas worst affected by overgrazing is the Sahel, a band of grassland across Africa just south of the Sahara Desert. The Sahel has been under heavy grazing pressure for thousands of years. The grasses that made it prime pastureland in ancient times have become rare plants: they now survive only as tiny clumps in rocky areas that livestock cannot reach.

Recent research has found that as much as two-thirds of the sparse rainfall in the Sahel consists of water evaporated from plants and the soil, not from the ocean. Overgrazing has removed the plants that provided much of the land's moisture, and erosion has reduced the ability of the soil to hold water. As a result there is still less evaporation, and less rainfall. Much of the area thus becomes desert.

DEBATE – Should farming techniques be changed to protect wildlife?

- Yes. Because it is important to maintain the biodiversity of agricultural land, and it is possible to farm land profitably in ways that will protect wildlife.
- No. Because intensive farming produces more food per acre, and we need to produce as much food as possible.

In this field in the USA, as on grassland farms around the world, the ground is completely cleared of other plants before crops are planted. There is no cover for animals, and no variety of plant life.

What Is The Value Of Wild Grasslands?

Humans have taken over most of the world's grasslands, but there are still a few wild areas that have not been affected by human activity. A few other areas, some very small, are being restored to their original condition. Although they are less dramatic than the rainforests, grasslands are just as valuable as other natural biomes.

GRASSLAND SOIL IS naturally very fertile, as the earliest farmers learned when they first grew crops and grazed cattle. They did not understand why the soil was so fertile, or how the fertility could be maintained. We now know a little better, largely from the study of wild grasslands.

The complex ecosystems of grasslands and their wide range of plants and animals have a lot to teach botanists and zoologists. Some grassland plants have

This lioness and her cubs will be safe for as long as grasslands like the Masai Mara, in Kenya, are worth more as a tourist destination than as agricultural land.

medicinal value. The plains-dwelling Native Americans used coneflower root as a painkiller and an antibiotic, in fact as a treatment for everything from snakebite to the common cold. It has been found to protect against viruses like influenza (flu), as well as stimulating the immune system. Coneflower is also an effective natural insecticide. European grasslands produce many medicinal plants, and these have been catalogued in herbals for hundreds of years.

This pastureland in Ohio, USA is full of cornflowers, both purple and grey-headed species. A meadow like this is not only beautiful but of great ecological value.

Where do wild grasslands survive?

The few remaining natural grasslands of the world have survived because they are too remote and inhospitable for people to have exploited them. Tussock grass on sub-Antarctic islands, for example, is beyond the reach of farmers, and the paramo is too high up to be over-exploited. Where humans can reach tussock grass, as in New Zealand, it is quickly destroyed, beyond the hope of being restored.

Wild grasslands survive only in sparsely populated areas like the Mongolian plains and the steppes of north-eastern Asia. Even there, they are occupied not by the original grazing animals but by the herds of domestic animals owned by nomadic herders. Large predators are everywhere under pressure, but in other ways these wild grasslands are much as they were before humans intervened.

In Africa, apart from the Sahel, wild grasslands are found in the belt of savannah that forms the setting for many TV features and safari holidays. This is what has saved the area from being farmed: the money it can raise from tourism makes it more valuable as a nature reserve than as farmland.

What about Europe?

There is no truly wild grassland left in Europe, because of human activities. The lowlands have been farmed for thousands of years. Alpine meadows, which are found on steep mountainsides across Europe, are not natural grasslands at all, but semi-natural pastures cleared from the forest hundreds of years ago. Celebrated grassland areas in Britain, such as the South Downs and Salisbury Plain, are also classified as 'semi-natural'. They were created in the sixth century, when Saxon invaders cut down the forests, and have been maintained since by grazing. Before this time, most of Britain was covered by forest.

This artificial landscape is very beautiful, and with good management a healthy wild flora and fauna can survive alongside intensive human agriculture. If grazing stopped for any reason – perhaps because it became uneconomic on the world market – the whole area would quickly revert to the shrubby woodland of pre-Saxon times, unless it were carefully managed to preserve it.

Does any wild prairie survive?

When Europeans arrived in North America, the prairies covered a quarter of the lower 48 states, and a large part of southern Canada. By the time farming had covered the continent, only small fragments of prairie remained. Illinois, the Prairie State, once contained 37 million acres of virgin prairie: there are now just 3500 acres (one ten-thousandth) left. In other states, where the prairie has not been ploughed it has become forest. This is because people are afraid of fire. If Europeans had followed the practice of the Native Americans, they would have burned the prairie – or let it burn when lightning set it on fire – to keep down the trees and encourage new grass.

The South American humid pampa is now all either pastureland or under the plough. The dry pampa survives in its wild state because it is unusable by farmers, though new irrigation techniques could threaten even such arid, unproductive land.

The plants growing on the limestone soil of Cressbrook Dale in Derbyshire, England are protected by law.

The world's smallest prairie

The Vermont Cemetery, in the outer
suburbs of Chicago, USA, can claim to
contain the world's smallest prairie.
One acre of the cemetery is
untouched ground, standing a foot
higher than the surrounding
cornfields. It survived because it is
hallowed ground. Ground squirrels
burrow among the old graves, and the
cemetery contains a wide range of
prairie flowers. Since 1975, seeds
collected from here have been
scattered on 450 acres of derelict
farmland nearby to recreate at least
the plant life of the local prairies. In
1989, the new prairie was declared a
national environmental research park,
to be the foundation stone of other
prairie reclamation efforts elsewhere.

*The prairie in western Kansas, USA, is
now a continuous sea of wheat fields.
The circles are created by enormous
irrigation machines.*

Can We Protect Grasslands?

With very few exceptions the remaining natural grasslands of the world survive only because people do not need them. For the time being they are safe, though they could be threatened in the future. The grasslands that need protection today are the semi-natural grasslands, where pressure from farming is increasing.

THE EXAMPLE OF the Vermont Cemetery shows that grassland can be protected. In that case it was almost accidental, because no one wanted to plough holy ground. It now produces seeds that are being used to replant and restore other prairie areas. These will have scientific and spiritual value, and will no doubt be there for future generations to enjoy.

Restoring grasslands in places where they have been damaged by overgrazing or over-intensive farming is a different matter. It would involve persuading the people living in the area to look elsewhere for grazing and food. It is hard to imagine a way of restoring the Sahel, for example, without somehow providing an alternative food supply for many thousands of people.

How can pastures be protected?

In countries where the population is not so poor, protecting semi-natural grassland is more feasible. Where farmers have enough land to move their flocks and herds to fresh pastures, leaving other areas to regrow, the grassland will survive indefinitely. A lot of grassland was lost in the 1950s in England because the demand for food after the Second World War meant that more land had to be ploughed; but since then, although there has been a steady decline in pasture, important grasslands such as the South Downs have been protected.

Military orchids now grow in more than one secret site: these are in a reserve belonging to the Suffolk Wildlife Trust.

The wonderful semi–natural alpine scenery of the Austrian Tyrol is maintained by government grants to the farmers, who use it to grow hay and feed cattle.

How are alpine pastures protected?

Alpine pastures in Austria and Switzerland are protected by local government, because they are recognised as a major tourist asset. Farmers cut hay in much the same way as their grandfathers did, often still using scythes (though some use small mechanical mowers), and dry it in huts in the mountain meadows. From there it is carried to the valleys to feed the cattle when they are taken down from the high pastures in winter. No pesticides are used anywhere in the mountains. The result is some of the best-preserved grassland in Europe, full of wildflowers, butterflies and grasshoppers – and a flourishing population of horseflies that feed on the cattle, and on passing walkers.

How can sheep protect a rare plant?

The military orchid was common on pastures in southern England in the nineteenth century, but by about 1914 it was thought to be extinct. In 1947 a botanist found a small group of the plants in the Chilterns, but he never told anyone where he found them. In the 1960s military orchids were discovered near Marlow in Buckinghamshire, in a place known only to a handful of people. At the end of the 1980s, when this site had 50 plants, it was opened to the public. Today, sheep graze on the land from time to time, to keep the grass at the length the orchid prefers.

Source: Flora Britannica *by Richard Mabey, 1996*

What are the pressures on the savannah?

The great national parks in Africa were originally set up as hunting reserves during the days of the British Empire. With independence, countries like Kenya, Tanzania, Zambia and Zimbabwe recognised that the parks and their wildlife attracted tourists, who brought much-needed money into the country. The newly independent African governments maintained the parks as a source of income. However, they are under pressure today from poaching – the illegal hunting of elephants for their ivory and rhinos for their horns, and also for 'bush meat', the meat of wild animals. Defending the parks against poaching needs money for wardens, which the governments can ill afford. Today, also, with rising populations in these countries, there is a heavy demand for new farming land, and hungry eyes are looking at the national parks. Outside the parks, little of the savannah survives, as we have seen. The national parks may be safe for the time being, but their survival will depend on continued income from tourism.

Tourism depends in its turn on safe and secure air travel. If people are scared to fly, or few people have the money to do so, the land may one day become more valuable as a place to grow food.

Tourists near the Victoria Falls in Zimbabwe visit a waterhole on elephant back.

A scientist extracts an ice core from the Antarctic ice sheet. The ice has been laid down over hundreds of years. By analysing the layers within the ice core, scientists can calculate levels of carbon dioxide in the atmosphere many years ago.

Will climate change affect grasslands?

The most serious long-term threat to grasslands may be the change in the global climate, which is thought by most scientists to be caused by rising levels of gases such as carbon dioxide in the atmosphere. The effect of this is not just to make the Earth warmer, but also to alter the patterns of rainfall worldwide. Places that are now too dry to support grasslands may well become wetter, but places where grass now grows – including farmland growing wheat and other human food crops – may become either too wet or too dry. Climate changes such as this have happened in the past – one of them gave rise to grasslands 65 million years ago, in the Cenozoic era. But in the past such changes took place over millions of years, giving plants time to evolve to meet the challenge. The changes in climate over the last 150 years or so have been too fast for the grasslands to adapt.

DEBATE - Should savannah grasslands be protected to preserve wildlife in an African country where people are short of food?

- Yes. Because wildlife reserves attract tourists, who bring foreign exchange into the country, and wild animals and plants must be protected from becoming extinct.
- No. Because growing food and exporting crops also earns money, and people are more important than animals.

What next for the world's grasslands?

Grasslands have a problem compared with other biomes: they are not visibly in danger, and they are not as glamorous as rainforests and oceans. Huge wheat fields look healthy: it is easy to overlook the habitat destruction that they represent. In contrast, overgrazed pastures seem beyond salvation: it seems easier to send food to the people whose pastureland has been ruined than to restore their pastures. It is possible to repair the damage done by centuries of misuse or neglect, if only the money can be found. A lot of research has been done, but to apply it needs action not by governments but by the people whose lives depend on the land.

The road to life: large, interconnected national parks allow long-distance migration by zebra and wildbeest in search of water and better grazing.

Can local action save grasslands?

The best chance for grasslands is at the local level. Overgrazing is a major cause of grassland destruction, and it is a local problem. Reducing the number of cattle in an area is not always possible, because in some places cattle are regarded as status symbols and people are not willing to give them up. Finding another source of food for the cattle has helped in some places, where it has been possible to grow trees and shrubs with nutritious leaves for the cattle to eat. Elsewhere, irrigation has helped to water grasslands that had become too dry to support cattle. Although only a few overgrazed pastures have been restored, this approach is better for the environment than abandoning ruined grasslands. It is not only the farmers who benefit, but all the animals and plants with which they share the land.

What effect will GM crops have?

Ever since the first farmers selected wild barley with the biggest seeds to plant for next season, people have been modifying the genetics of crop plants. They have bred strains of potatoes and grapes that are resistant to disease and the attacks of insects. Now, though, scientists have found ways of changing the genetics of plants more directly, rather than through selective breeding. They can 'design' plants that are immune to a herbicide (weedkiller), so that farmers can use large amounts of herbicide to kill off weeds without affecting the crop plant. Other crop plants have been genetically modified to be resistant to pests, and this can lead to big reductions in the use of pesticides and the increase of wildlife.

In the UK, fields of GM crops are being grown as part of scientific tests. Anti-GM campaigners have invaded several of these fields to protest against the tests. They believe that the GM crops could spread beyond the test areas and contaminate other crops.

Some genetically modified plants produce sterile seeds, which are good for food but will not grow into new plants. This is a great advantage to people selling seed, because farmers have to buy new seeds every year and cannot store some seeds for planting next season. However it is a great disadvantage to farmers, especially in poor countries. Also, if such plants were to form hybrids with wild plants, it could have serious effects on grasslands.

REFERENCE

GRASSLAND CHARACTERISTICS

- Prairies are divided into three types: short-grass, long-grass and mixed or mid-grass.

- Short-grass prairies grow in the west, in the rain shadow of the Rocky Mountains, where the rainfall averages 300 mm. Their grass cover is made up of drought-tolerant species, growing to about 15–30 cm tall.

- Long-grass prairies occupy the eastern third of the area, where the rainfall averages about 900 mm per year. The grasses here grow to 2–4m tall.

- The area between the two is known as mid-grass prairie, where grass height varies with local weather and topography.

- Tropical grasslands grow where there is a marked difference between wet and dry seasons. The dry season is usually longer than the wet, and is between 2 and 11 months long.

- Savannah grows within 8° and 20° of the Equator. There is between 800 and 1500 mm of rain per year, and rainfall is strongly seasonal. The three types are wet savannah, where the dry season is between three and five months, dry savannah, where the dry season is five to seven months, and thornbush, the driest type, where long droughts are frequent.

- Temperate grasslands grow where rainfall is between 250 and 750 mm per year. The rain falls throughout the year rather than in one season.

CROPS FROM GRASSES

- **Rye:** used as a bread grain and livestock feed; also used in distillation of whisky and gin. First cultivated 2000–3000 years ago, still grown in northern Europe and Asia.

- **Wheat:** used as a bread grain. First cultivated 9000 years ago from wild einkorn, and wild emmer. Emmer was the wheat used by the Greeks and Romans.

- **Oats:** used as a cereal food and cattle feed; also oat straw is used as animal bedding. First cultivated about 4500 years ago.

- **Rice:** used as a food grain; also used in distillation of wine and spirits. Cultivation originated as early as 10 000 BC in Asia. There is archaeological evidence of rice growing in Thailand in 4000 BC, from where it spread to China, Japan, and Indonesia. By 400 BC rice was cultivated in the Middle East and Africa. Introduced to Greece and nearby Mediterranean countries around 330 BC. Brought to the American colonies in the early 1600s, commercial production began in 1685.

- **Maize (corn):** used as a food grain; also used for bread. The staple grain of the Americas for many centuries before Europeans reached the New World. Has been cultivated in the south-western United States for at least 3000 years. Early wild corn was not much different from the modern corn plant.

- **Sorghum (milo):** used as a food grain, mainly in Africa, and as livestock feed in USA. Also used to make beer and adhesive. Probably first cultivated 7000 years ago in north-east Africa. Taken to America in nineteenth century.

PERCENTAGE OF GRAIN CONSUMED BY HUMANS AND BY ANIMALS

Area	Humans	Animals
Africa	83	15
Asia	80	16
Latin America	49	39
European Union	28	41
USA	22	48

PRODUCTIVITY OF THE EARTH'S MAJOR HABITATS

HABITAT	MASS OF PLANTS PRODUCED (grams per square metre per year)
Forests:	
tropical	1800
temperate	1250
boreal (cold)	800
Swamp and marsh	2500
Savannah	700
Cultivated land	650
Shrubland	600
Desert scrub	70
Temperate grassland	500
Tundra and alpine	140
Aquatic habitats:	
algal beds and reefs	2000
estuaries	1800
lakes and streams	500
continental shelf	360
open ocean	125

(Source: Adapted from Robert E. Ricklefs, Ecology, 3rd edition, copyright 1990 by W.H. Freeman and Company, used with permission)

EFFECTS OF CLIMATE CHANGE

- In the mid-1950s Charles Keeling, a scientist at the University of California, began measuring the amount of carbon dioxide (CO_2) in the air. He found that because the atmosphere is so thoroughly mixed by winds, the carbon dioxide concentration was the same wherever he measured it.

- In 1958 the concentration of carbon dioxide in the air was 315 parts per million (ppm). Since then, CO_2 levels have been measured every year at Mauna Loa in Hawaii.

- The graph below shows how CO_2 levels have changed over time. The 'Keeling curve', as it is known, shows that CO_2 levels have risen steadily, through 336 ppm in 1980 to over 350 ppm in 2000.

(Source: 'Wet, Wet, Wet' by Brian Cathcart, The Times Magazine, 7 September 2002)

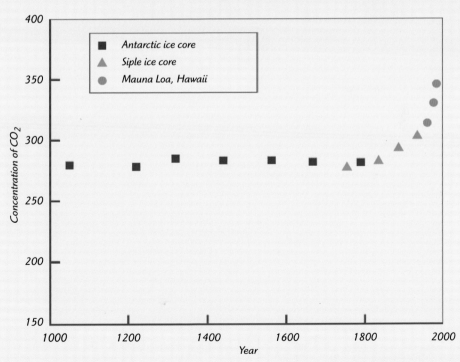

CHANGES IN CO_2 LEVELS SINCE AD 1000

GLOSSARY

aerate To break up the soil so that air can get in.

annual A plant that grows, produces seed and dies within a season.

apical shoot A shoot at the tip of a plant.

bacteria Microscopic living things that are neither plants nor animals.

browse Leaves and the young shoots of shrubs and trees, eaten by cattle and other animals.

carnivorous A carnivorous animal eats other animals for food.

chitin The hard substance that covers insect bodies.

classified When living things are sorted into groups and given names, based on their relationships.

ecology The scientific study of animals and plants in their natural surroundings.

enamel The hard substance that forms the outer layer of teeth.

erosion Wearing away, either of teeth or of soil and rocks.

fermentation The breaking down of food by the action of bacteria or yeasts (microscopic fungi).

genus A group of closely related species.

germinate To grow, like a seed.

grazing Eating grass.

herbal A book that lists many types of plants and their uses.

herbivores Animals that eat plants.

hybrid A combination, sometimes called a cross, between two different plants or animals.

larva (plural larvae) The first stage in the life of an insect, after hatching from the egg.

migrate To travel regularly to find more suitable conditions.

mollusc Any of a group of animals that are soft-bodied and often have shells. They include slugs, snails, clams, mussels, squids and octopuses.

perennial A plant that lives on from year to year.

predator An animal that hunts and kills other animals.

rain shadow An area that gets little rain because it is on the landward side of a range of mountains, and most rain falls on the seaward slopes of the mountains.

ruminant An animal that re-chews its food ('chews the cud'), such as a cow or a deer.

rumination Re-chewing food that has been swallowed once already.

silage Grass that is stored wet and allowed to ferment, and is then used for animal feed.

species A group of similar animals or plants that can breed together naturally and produce normal offspring.

staple The main item in the diet of a human or other animal.

yurt (also called a ger) A type of tent made of felt or skins, used by nomadic peoples in Mongolia and central Asia.

FURTHER INFORMATION

BOOKS

Grassland: the History, Biology, Politics and Promise of the American Prairie by Richard Manning (Penguin Books, 1997)
Highly recommended. The effect of different methods of agriculture in the USA, illustrated by stories old and new, with an unexpected conclusion.

European Wet Grassland by P. Jose Benstead (RSPB, 1999)
A survey of bird life in a wide variety of grassland habitats in Europe, with implications for grassland ecology worldwide.

Grassland and Heathland Habitats by Elizabeth Price (Routledge, 2002)
A detailed account of the ecology of these treeless areas as homes for animals and plants.

Living on a Plain by Joanne Winne (Children's Press, 2000)
For younger readers: a description of the American prairie as it affects the people who live there.

Grasslands (First Reports) by Susan Heinrichs Gray (Compass Point, 2001)
The ecology of grasslands in the USA, for school-age readers. Part of a useful series of biome-centered books.

African Grasslands by Christina Longman (Peter Bedrick, 2001)
An introduction for younger readers to the complex and dramatic ecosystem of the African savannah.

Endangered Grasslands by J. David Taylor (Crabtree, 1991)
A survey of threatened grasslands, with the reasons for their present endangered status.

Grasses: An Identification Guide by Lauren Brown (Houghton Mifflin, 1992)
An eye-opening book, revealing the beauty and complexity of an often overlooked family of plants.

The Feather and the Furrow by Chris Knights (Merlin Unwin, 2002)
A personal account of an English farmer's lifelong efforts to protect and improve the wildlife habitats on his farm.

The Little House on the Prairie by Laura Ingalls Wilder (Penguin, 2003)
Although this is a fictional account of a family's move to the American prairie in the mid-nineteenth century, the story gives the reader a good idea of what it was like to live on the prairie at this time.

A Painted House by John Grisham (Arrow Books, 2001)
A very good book that gives a vivid picture of farm life in Arkansas. Be warned that some parts of the book are quite gory.

ORGANIZATIONS

Fauna and Flora International
Great Eastern House, Tenison Road
Cambridge CB1 2TT, UK
A world-wide organization with a huge
range of conservation projects, many
involving grasslands. Serious scientific
reports, together with up-to-date news
of current projects.
Website: www.fauna-flora.org

National Wildlife Foundation
11100 Wildlife Center Drive, Reston
VA 20190-5362, USA
A US-based conservation organization.
They have an excellent website with
conservation and action pages about
prairie grasslands, a newsroom and a
guide to environmental activities.
There is also a special children's and
teen section.
Website: www.nwf.org/kids

Worldwide Fund for Nature
Panda House, Weyside Park
Godalming, Surrey GU2 1XR, UK
An international organization covering
much the same ground as National
Wildlife Foundation, with a similar
range of news and action lines.
Website: www.wwf-uk.org

WEBSITES

**www.mobot.org/MBGnet/sets/grasslnd
/index.htm**
This simple site has information about
grasslands, particularly grassland plants
and animals, and links to other
grassland websites.

www.prairiesource.com
This site about the American prairie
includes a wildflower guide and a
screensaver.

www.nwf.org/grasslands/
The US National Wildlife Federation's
site on grasslands, with information
about buffalo, prairie dogs and sage
grouse.

VISIT

Rothamstead Research Station
Harpenden, Hertfordshire
The oldest continuous grassland
management experiment in the world.
Wonderful wildflower meadows in
spring and summer.

INDEX